I thirst

— JOHN 19:28

Fr. Mark Goring is a member of the Companions of the Cross, an order of priests based in Ottawa, Ontario.

He joined the Companions of the Cross when he was 18 and was ordained to the priesthood in 2002, at age 26.

To learn more about our priests & seminarians, to discover the spirituality, brotherhood & mission of the Companions of the Cross and how you can participate, and to find more prayer resources, please visit:
www.companionscross.org

CONTENTS

WE ARE ALL

Searching

FOR SOMETHING MORE

We want to know the purpose of our lives and what leads to true fulfillment.

We desire to love and be loved.

What is life all about?

Is there something more?

God's Love

You were created for relationship with God. God created you, knows you, and loves you personally. He sees you as his child, and he will never stop loving you. God is love. He is good and has your best interests at heart. God can be trusted and is constantly working for your good.

God

You

a. Created for relationship (1 John 3:1)

b. God loves you (Isaiah 43:1-5)

c. God's love is never-ending (Isaiah 54:10)

d. He has a plan for you (Jeremiah 29:11-13)

We Have Sinned

The unity of this loving relationship we were created for has been damaged. Something has come between God and us: sin. We have all sinned and turned away from God. Sin has real consequences. It harms our relationship with God, with others, and with ourselves.

a. Our relationship
   is broken
   (Isaiah 59:2)
b. We are lost and
   without hope
   (Romans 6:23a)

Good News

God loves us so much that he could not bear to be separated from us. He sent his son Jesus to restore our relationship with him. When Jesus was nailed to the cross, he took upon himself all the consequences of our sins, and by his rising from the dead brought us new life. Jesus alone restores our relationship with God and bridges the gap caused by sin.

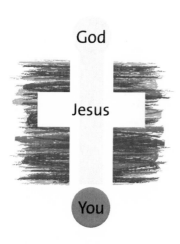

a. Jesus restores our relationship (John 3:16)
b. God saves because he loves us (Romans 5:8)
c. Jesus is the only way to God (1 Tim 2:5, John 14:6)
d. In the Church we have communion with Jesus (Acts 2:31-47, 1 Corinthians 12:12-13, Ephesians 4:1-6)
e. Promise of Heaven! (1 Peter 1:3-5, Rev 21:1-4)

Your Response

You can experience this restored relationship! The Good News of Jesus is wonderful, but it remains outside of us until we make a response. We must make a choice. God is like a man proposing – down on one knee waiting patiently, hoping beyond hope that you will say "yes" and give him your whole heart.

God
Jesus
You

a. Repent
   (1 John 1:8-9)
b. Believe
   (Romans 10:9-13)
c. Be Baptized
   (Acts 2:38)

Prayer of Surrender

Whether you have been close or far from him in the past, he is waiting for you to open the door. Take a moment to look at the following prayer:

> *"Lord Jesus, I believe that you know me and love me. I have not always chosen to love you, and have broken my relationship with you through my sins. Thank you for proving your love for me on the cross so that our relationship can be restored. I open the door of my heart and invite you to be at the centre of my life – to be my Saviour and my Lord. Direct me and help me to live the Gospel with my whole life. Amen."*

Would you like to invite Jesus to be at the centre of your life? Will you choose Jesus and give God permission?

If so, step out in faith and pray to him right now.

IF WE LET CHRIST INTO OUR LIVES, WE LOSE NOTHING.

- POPE BENEDICT XVI

Introduction

This book is a prayer guide that will lead you into a personal relationship with the Holy Trinity.

God is our treasure, and yet few people embark on the adventure of seeking God. Scripture promises that if we seek the Lord we will find him.

This book is a 40-day challenge. The challenge is to pray 10 minutes a day for 40 days.

My hope is that through this book you will acquire the discipline of daily prayer and that this discipline will remain with you for the rest of your life.

– Fr. Mark Goring, CC

HOW TO USE

Treasure

IN

Heaven

In the next 40 days, we will be incorporating different elements into our daily ten minute prayer reflection. This structure will give you a solid foundation that you can use to build your own personal prayer life. The elements can be categorized as such:

1. Seven prayers that I believe are essential to the prayer life of every Catholic.

2. A scripture passage to reflect on each day.

3. Inviting the Holy Spirit to lead you in prayer.

4. Thanksgiving and intercessions.

5. Freedom Prayer.

6. Journaling.

I will go over the specific structure of the daily prayer time on page 22.

Seven Prayers

There are seven prayers I believe every Catholic should pray daily. They are included in this booklet and are as follows:

1. **The Daily Offering** is a prayer entrusting all that we have and are to the Lord. I have included my favourite one in this booklet.

2. **The Our Father** is the prayer that Jesus taught his disciples when they asked him how to pray.

3. **The Hail Mary** is the prayer Catholics most commonly use to honour Mary our Mother and to ask for her intercession.

4. **The Doxology** is a prayer of worship and adoration to God who is Father, Son and Holy Spirit.

5. **The Act of Contrition** is a prayer of repentance asking God for his mercy and forgiveness.

6. **The Guardian Angel Prayer** reminds us that we have an angel constantly watching over us and invokes his help.

7. **St. Michael the Archangel Prayer** reminds us that we are in a spiritual battle. By invoking St. Michael we receive help against the forces of darkness.

40 Scriptures

This booklet includes 40 scripture passages. Meditate on one each day. Meditating on scripture is similar to pondering a piece of art; it is important that you take your time. Stay with the scripture until it makes an impression on you. I usually meditate on the scripture of the day for about three minutes.

Letting the
Holy Spirit
lead you in Prayer

Pray each prayer slowly with an awareness of God's presence. Allow the Holy Spirit to speak to your heart during your time of meditating on scripture.

Do not go through the time of thanksgiving and intercession routinely. Allow the Holy Spirit to lead and inspire you when you are thinking of what to pray for. Within a short time you will notice the Holy Spirit teaching you how to pray.

Freedom Prayer

Included in this booklet is a prayer for freedom (on Page 26). Take 40 days to ask God to set you free from an area of sinfulness or weakness in your life.

How the Freedom Prayer Works

1. **Small Steps** - Most things grow slowly. Choose something attainable when deciding in what area of your life to ask the Lord for freedom.

2. **Virtue Begets Virtue** - By gaining freedom in one small area of your life you will experience a positive "ripple effect" in many other areas of your life.

3. **Ask the Holy Spirit** - The Holy Spirit can help you pinpoint the one small change in your life that has the potential of impacting your whole life for the better. Ask the Holy Spirit to show you what small change will best improve your life.

4. **40 Days** - 40 days is the perfect amount of time to break the power of a bad habit or to form a good habit in our lives.

FR. BOB ON JOURNALING

A lot of people shy away from the suggestion that they should consider keeping personal journals. It must be because they misunderstand what is involved, or maybe these are the people who once tried to maintain diaries and found they could not stay with it. A journal is not a diary.

A spiritual journal is related to my time of personal prayer, my daily quiet time with the Lord. Whatever writing I decide to do in it can ordinarily be done during prayer time. In fact, many people refer to these little notebooks as their prayer journals.

To my prayer journal I can commit my promises to the Lord. I can write in my requests. I can thank him for blessings, for specific answers to petitions. I can summarize my day, include reflections on what I sense God may be saying to me, and record resolutions I make as to how I should respond. I can register my complaints. Among the things I think I've learned about the Lord is that he likes me to complain to him. He doesn't want me to complain to others, but he likes to give me the chance to get things off my chest in conversation with him. He can handle it. Even if I'm a bit angry with him, he doesn't mind my writing that down either. He is totally unthreatened by my annoyance. He knows allowing me to express it can be quite therapeutic for me. All of these things and more I can record in my journal.

It may sound like a lot, but it really isn't. Five minutes a day should take care of it. Some days maybe nothing needs to be written.

The value of the prayer journal is, perhaps, two-fold writing things down may help me to get my thoughts into focus and keeping a record of how my relationship with the Lord is progressing can be a very useful reminder as time goes on.

We are all eager to catch the Lord's word. We want to know what he is saying to us. Very often, as we continue to pursue his will, we forget what he has already said. If we are faithful to journaling, we'll have the record we need. I get the impression God doesn't say everything at once. Probably to keep us seeking him, he will give us his word a bit at a time. If we don't keep a record of it, we are liable to forget it.

It is useful, I find, in writing in my journal, to address God in the first person. I write directly to him, to the Father. That way, it keeps me in prayer, keeps me communicating with him.

Over the past few years, I have been reasonably faithful to the practice of keeping a journal. There were a couple of extended periods, however, when I just let it go and didn't bother. I have lived to regret it. I have looked back on those unrecorded times and wondered again and again what was happening in my life. I can't remember. I've lost it.

In order to make journaling most effective, I have to do a regular review. Every couple of months serves to keep me up to date.

A well-kept journal will be like a folio of personal correspondence with the Lord. Keeping such a record can be a very valuable help to anyone who wants to grow into a closer union with him.

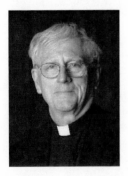

Fr. Bob Bedard, CC was the Founder of the Companions of the Cross.

He is fondly remembered for his unparalleled passion for the Lord, his gentle fatherly care, and incredible sense of humour.

He passed on to his eternal reward on October 6, 2011.

THE DAILY

Structure

I highly recommend that you mark this section so that you can easily reference it during your prayer time.

We will start and end our time of prayer by making the sign of the cross. Using your right hand, gently touch your forehead, then chest, then your left shoulder, and then your right shoulder to trace a cross over yourself while saying these words:

In the Name of the Father,
and of the Son,
and of the Holy Spirit. Amen.

+

INVITING THE HOLY SPIRIT
Holy Spirit, teach me how to pray.

+

DAILY OFFERING
O my Jesus,
through the Immaculate Heart of Mary,
I offer You all my prayers, works,
joys and sufferings of this day,
in union with the Holy Sacrifice of the Mass
throughout the world,
in thanksgiving for Your goodness to me,
in reparation for my sins,
for the intentions of my family and friends,
and those who have asked me to pray for them
and for our Holy Father, the Pope. Amen.

+

OUR FATHER

Our Father, Who art in heaven,
Hallowed be Thy Name.
Thy Kingdom come.
Thy Will be done, on earth as it is in Heaven.
Give us this day our daily bread.
And forgive us our trespasses,
as we forgive those who trespass against us.
And lead us not into temptation,
but deliver us from evil. Amen.

✝

HAIL MARY

Hail Mary, Full of Grace,
The Lord is with thee.
Blessed art thou among women,
and blessed is the fruit
of thy womb, Jesus.
Holy Mary, Mother of God,
pray for us sinners now,
and at the hour of our death. Amen.

✝

DOXOLOGY

Glory be to the Father,
and to the Son,
and to the Holy Spirit.
As it was in the beginning,
is now, and ever shall be,
world without end. Amen.

✝

*(Think of three things for which to
ask the Lord's forgiveness)*

+

ACT OF CONTRITION
O my God,
I am heartily sorry for
having offended You,
and I detest all my sins,
because I dread the loss of heaven,
and the pains of hell;
but most of all because
they offend You, my God,
Who are all good and
deserving of all my love.
I firmly resolve,
with the help of Your grace,
to confess my sins,
to do penance,
and to amend my life. Amen.

+

DAILY SCRIPTURE REFLECTION, JOURNALING, THANKSGIVING, INTERCESSIONS
*(Read the daily scripture passage, and take a
couple of minutes to reflect on it. Read it again slowly
and focus on a word or phrase that stands out to you.
Take this time to journal whatever is on your heart. You
will also find space to write down three things you are
thankful for and three things for God's help.)*

+

FREEDOM PRAYER
Lord Jesus Christ, Son of God,
have mercy on me a sinner.
You promised Lord that You
would set the captives free.
I confess Jesus that I am a slave and
only You can break the chains that bind me.
I repent of relying on my own strength.
Without You Jesus I can do nothing.
I ask You Lord Jesus to set me free from

(*name an area in your life
where you need freedom*).

Come now Holy Spirit and
clothe me with power from on high.

(*take a moment and allow the
Holy Spirit to empower you*)

Give me the grace Lord Jesus to walk in faith today,
confident in Your love and mercy. Amen.

+

GUARDIAN ANGEL
Angel of God,
my guardian dear,
To whom God's love
commits me here,
Ever this day,
be at my side,
To light and guard,
To rule and guide. Amen.

+

ST. MICHAEL THE ARCHANGEL PRAYER

St. Michael the Archangel,
defend us in battle.
Be our defense against the wickedness
and snares of the devil.
May God rebuke him, we humbly pray,
and do thou, O Prince of the heavenly hosts, by the
power of God, thrust into hell Satan,
and all the evil spirits, who prowl about the world
seeking the ruin of souls. Amen.

+

In the Name of the Father,
and of the Son,
and of the Holy Spirit. Amen.

+

DAILY Scripture REFLECTION

KEEPING TRACK

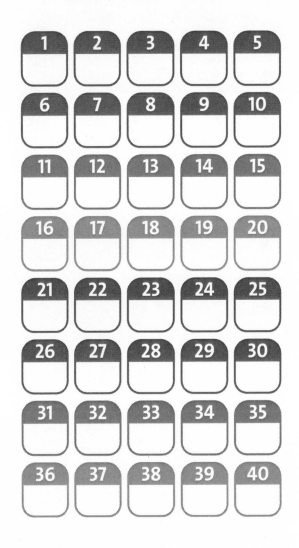

WE CAN KNOW GOD

(DAYS 1-5)

SIGN OF THE CROSS

INVITING THE HOLY SPIRIT

DAILY OFFERING PRAYER

OUR FATHER

HAIL MARY

DOXOLOGY

ACT OF CONTRITION

DAILY SCRIPTURE REFLECTION

JOURNALING

THANKSGIVING

INTERCESSIONS

FREEDOM PRAYER

GUARDIAN ANGEL

ST. MICHAEL THE ARCHANGEL PRAYER

SIGN OF THE CROSS

DAY 1

You will seek me and find me; when you seek me with all your heart.

– Jeremiah 29:13

The Daily Structure can be found on Pg. 22

THANKSGIVING

What three things are you thankful for today?

_____

_____

_____

_____

_____

_____

INTERCESSIONS

What three things do you want to ask for God's help?

_____

_____

_____

_____

_____

_____

_____

WE CAN KNOW GOD

DAY 1

WE CAN KNOW GOD

SIGN OF
THE CROSS

INVITING THE
HOLY SPIRIT

DAILY
OFFERING
PRAYER

OUR FATHER

HAIL MARY

DOXOLOGY

ACT OF
CONTRITION

DAILY
SCRIPTURE
REFLECTION

JOURNALING

THANKSGIVING

INTERCESSIONS

FREEDOM
PRAYER

GUARDIAN
ANGEL

ST. MICHAEL
THE
ARCHANGEL
PRAYER

SIGN OF
THE CROSS

DAY 2

*Ask, and it will be given you;
seek, and you will find; knock,
and it will be opened to you.*

– Matthew 7:7

The Daily Structure can be found on Pg. 22

THANKSGIVING

What three things are you thankful for today?

_____

_____

_____

_____

_____

_____

INTERCESSIONS

What three things do you want to ask for God's help?

_____

_____

_____

_____

_____

_____

_____

WE CAN KNOW GOD

DAY 2

WE CAN KNOW GOD
(DAYS 1-5)

SIGN OF
THE CROSS

INVITING THE
HOLY SPIRIT

DAILY
OFFERING
PRAYER

OUR FATHER

HAIL MARY

DOXOLOGY

ACT OF
CONTRITION

DAILY
SCRIPTURE
REFLECTION

JOURNALING

THANKSGIVING

INTERCESSIONS

FREEDOM
PRAYER

GUARDIAN
ANGEL

ST. MICHAEL
THE
ARCHANGEL
PRAYER

SIGN OF
THE CROSS

DAY 3

But to all who received him, who believed in his name, he gave power to become children of God.

– John 1:12

The Daily Structure can be found on Pg. 22

THANKSGIVING

What three things are you thankful for today?

_____

_____

_____

_____

_____

_____

INTERCESSIONS

What three things do you want to ask for God's help?

_____

_____

_____

_____

_____

_____

_____

WE CAN KNOW GOD

DAY 3

WE CAN KNOW GOD

(DAYS 1-5)

SIGN OF
THE CROSS

INVITING THE
HOLY SPIRIT

DAILY
OFFERING
PRAYER

OUR FATHER

HAIL MARY

DOXOLOGY

ACT OF
CONTRITION

DAILY
SCRIPTURE
REFLECTION

JOURNALING

THANKSGIVING

INTERCESSIONS

FREEDOM
PRAYER

GUARDIAN
ANGEL

ST. MICHAEL
THE
ARCHANGEL
PRAYER

SIGN OF
THE CROSS

DAY 4

See what love the Father has given us, that we should be called children of God; and so we are.

– 1 John 3:1

The Daily Structure can be found on Pg. 22

THANKSGIVING

What three things are you thankful for today?

_____

_____

_____

_____

_____

_____

INTERCESSIONS

What three things do you want to ask for God's help?

_____

_____

_____

_____

_____

_____

_____

WE CAN KNOW GOD

Day 4

WE CAN KNOW GOD

(DAYS 1-5)

SIGN OF
THE CROSS

INVITING THE
HOLY SPIRIT

DAILY
OFFERING
PRAYER

OUR FATHER

HAIL MARY

DOXOLOGY

ACT OF
CONTRITION

DAILY
SCRIPTURE
REFLECTION

JOURNALING

THANKSGIVING

INTERCESSIONS

FREEDOM
PRAYER

GUARDIAN
ANGEL

ST. MICHAEL
THE
ARCHANGEL
PRAYER

SIGN OF
THE CROSS

DAY 5

Draw near to God and he will draw near to you.

– James 4:8

The Daily Structure can be found on Pg. 22

THANKSGIVING

What three things are you thankful for today?

_____

_____

_____

_____

_____

_____

INTERCESSIONS

What three things do you want to ask for God's help?

_____

_____

_____

_____

_____

_____

_____

WE CAN KNOW GOD

DAY 5

GOD'S CARE

SIGN OF
THE CROSS

INVITING THE
HOLY SPIRIT

DAILY
OFFERING
PRAYER

OUR FATHER

HAIL MARY

DOXOLOGY

ACT OF
CONTRITION

DAILY
SCRIPTURE
REFLECTION

JOURNALING

THANKSGIVING

INTERCESSIONS

FREEDOM
PRAYER

GUARDIAN
ANGEL

ST. MICHAEL
THE
ARCHANGEL
PRAYER

SIGN OF
THE CROSS

DAY 6

Come to me, all who labour and are heavy laden, and I will give you rest. Take my yoke upon you, and learn from me; for I am gentle and lowly in heart, and you will find rest for your souls. For my yoke is easy, and my burden is light.

– Matthew 11:28-30

The Daily Structure can be found on Pg. 22

THANKSGIVING

What three things are you thankful for today?

_____

_____

_____

_____

_____

_____

INTERCESSIONS

What three things do you want to ask for God's help?

_____

_____

_____

_____

_____

_____

GOD'S CARE

DAY 6

GOD'S CARE

SIGN OF
THE CROSS

INVITING THE
HOLY SPIRIT

DAILY
OFFERING
PRAYER

OUR FATHER

HAIL MARY

DOXOLOGY

ACT OF
CONTRITION

DAILY
SCRIPTURE
REFLECTION

JOURNALING

THANKSGIVING

INTERCESSIONS

FREEDOM
PRAYER

GUARDIAN
ANGEL

ST. MICHAEL
THE
ARCHANGEL
PRAYER

SIGN OF
THE CROSS

DAY 7

The thief comes only to steal and kill and destroy; I came that they may have life, and have it abundantly.

– John 10:10

The Daily Structure can be found on Pg. 22

THANKSGIVING

What three things are you thankful for today?

INTERCESSIONS

What three things do you want to ask for God's help?

GOD'S CARE

DAY 7

GOD'S CARE
(DAYS 6-10)

DAY 8

Therefore I tell you, do not be anxious about your life, what you shall eat or what you shall drink, nor about your body, what you shall put on. Is not life more than food, and the body more than clothing? Look at the birds of the air: they neither sow nor reap nor gather into barns, and yet your heavenly Father feeds them. Are you not of more value than they?

– Matthew 6:25-26

The Daily Structure can be found on Pg. 22

THANKSGIVING

What three things are you thankful for today?

_____

_____

_____

_____

_____

_____

INTERCESSIONS

What three things do you want to ask for God's help?

_____

_____

_____

_____

_____

_____

_____

GOD'S CARE
DAY 8

GOD'S CARE

SIGN OF
THE CROSS

INVITING THE
HOLY SPIRIT

DAILY
OFFERING
PRAYER

OUR FATHER

HAIL MARY

DOXOLOGY

ACT OF
CONTRITION

DAILY
SCRIPTURE
REFLECTION

JOURNALING

THANKSGIVING

INTERCESSIONS

FREEDOM
PRAYER

GUARDIAN
ANGEL

ST. MICHAEL
THE
ARCHANGEL
PRAYER

SIGN OF
THE CROSS

DAY 9

*I am with you always, to
the close of the age.*

– Matthew 28:20

The Daily Structure can be found on Pg. 22

THANKSGIVING

What three things are you thankful for today?

_____

_____

_____

_____

_____

INTERCESSIONS

What three things do you want to ask for God's help?

_____

_____

_____

_____

_____

_____

GOD'S CARE

DAY 9

GOD'S CARE
(DAYS 6-10)

SIGN OF
THE CROSS

INVITING THE
HOLY SPIRIT

DAILY
OFFERING
PRAYER

OUR FATHER

HAIL MARY

DOXOLOGY

ACT OF
CONTRITION

DAILY
SCRIPTURE
REFLECTION

JOURNALING

THANKSGIVING

INTERCESSIONS

FREEDOM
PRAYER

GUARDIAN
ANGEL

ST. MICHAEL
THE
ARCHANGEL
PRAYER

SIGN OF
THE CROSS

DAY 10

Be not afraid.

– Luke 2:10

The Daily Structure can be found on Pg. 22

THANKSGIVING

What three things are you thankful for today?

_____

_____

_____

_____

_____

_____

INTERCESSIONS

What three things do you want to ask for God's help?

_____

_____

_____

_____

_____

_____

_____

GOD'S CARE

DAY 10

GOD'S FORGIVENESS
(DAYS 11-15)

SIGN OF
THE CROSS

INVITING THE
HOLY SPIRIT

DAILY
OFFERING
PRAYER

OUR FATHER

HAIL MARY

DOXOLOGY

ACT OF
CONTRITION

DAILY
SCRIPTURE
REFLECTION

JOURNALING

THANKSGIVING

INTERCESSIONS

FREEDOM
PRAYER

GUARDIAN
ANGEL

ST. MICHAEL
THE
ARCHANGEL
PRAYER

SIGN OF
THE CROSS

DAY 11

A new heart I will give you, and a new spirit I will put within you; and I will take out of your flesh the heart of stone and give you a heart of flesh.

– Ezekiel 36:26

The Daily Structure can be found on Pg. 22

THANKSGIVING

What three things are you thankful for today?

_____

_____

_____

_____

_____

_____

INTERCESSIONS

What three things do you want to ask for God's help?

_____

_____

_____

_____

_____

_____

_____

GOD'S FORGIVENESS

DAY 11

GOD'S FORGIVENESS
(DAYS 11-15)

DAY 12

Come now, let us reason together, says the LORD: though your sins are like scarlet, they shall be as white as snow; though they are red like crimson, they shall become like wool.

– Isaiah 1:18

The Daily Structure can be found on Pg. 22

THANKSGIVING

What three things are you thankful for today?

_____

_____

_____

_____

_____

_____

INTERCESSIONS

What three things do you want to ask for God's help?

_____

_____

_____

_____

_____

_____

_____

GOD'S FORGIVENESS

DAY 12

GOD'S FORGIVENESS

**SIGN OF
THE CROSS**

**INVITING THE
HOLY SPIRIT**

**DAILY
OFFERING
PRAYER**

OUR FATHER

HAIL MARY

DOXOLOGY

**ACT OF
CONTRITION**

**DAILY
SCRIPTURE
REFLECTION**

JOURNALING

THANKSGIVING

INTERCESSIONS

**FREEDOM
PRAYER**

**GUARDIAN
ANGEL**

**ST. MICHAEL
THE
ARCHANGEL
PRAYER**

**SIGN OF
THE CROSS**

DAY 13

*Neither do I condemn you;
go, and do not sin again.*

– John 8:11

The Daily Structure can be found on Pg. 22

THANKSGIVING

What three things are you thankful for today?

INTERCESSIONS

What three things do you want to ask for God's help?

GOD'S FORGIVENESS

DAY 13

SIGN OF THE CROSS

INVITING THE HOLY SPIRIT

DAILY OFFERING PRAYER

OUR FATHER

HAIL MARY

DOXOLOGY

ACT OF CONTRITION

DAILY SCRIPTURE REFLECTION

JOURNALING

THANKSGIVING

INTERCESSIONS

FREEDOM PRAYER

GUARDIAN ANGEL

ST. MICHAEL THE ARCHANGEL PRAYER

SIGN OF THE CROSS

DAY 14

There is therefore now no condemnation for those who are in Christ Jesus.

– Romans 8:1

The Daily Structure can be found on Pg. 22

THANKSGIVING

What three things are you thankful for today?

_____

_____

_____

_____

_____

INTERCESSIONS

What three things do you want to ask for God's help?

_____

_____

_____

_____

_____

_____

GOD'S FORGIVENESS

DAY 14

SIGN OF
THE CROSS

INVITING THE
HOLY SPIRIT

DAILY
OFFERING
PRAYER

OUR FATHER

HAIL MARY

DOXOLOGY

ACT OF
CONTRITION

DAILY
SCRIPTURE
REFLECTION

JOURNALING

THANKSGIVING

INTERCESSIONS

FREEDOM
PRAYER

GUARDIAN
ANGEL

ST. MICHAEL
THE
ARCHANGEL
PRAYER

SIGN OF
THE CROSS

DAY 15

There will be more joy in heaven over one sinner who repents than over ninety-nine righteous persons who need no repentance.

– Luke 15:7

The Daily Structure can be found on Pg. 22

THANKSGIVING

What three things are you thankful for today?

_____

_____

_____

_____

_____

_____

INTERCESSIONS

What three things do you want to ask for God's help?

_____

_____

_____

_____

_____

_____

GOD'S FORGIVENESS

DAY 15

JESUS CHRIST
(DAYS 16-20)

SIGN OF
THE CROSS

INVITING THE
HOLY SPIRIT

DAILY
OFFERING
PRAYER

OUR FATHER

HAIL MARY

DOXOLOGY

ACT OF
CONTRITION

DAILY
SCRIPTURE
REFLECTION

JOURNALING

THANKSGIVING

INTERCESSIONS

FREEDOM
PRAYER

GUARDIAN
ANGEL

ST. MICHAEL
THE
ARCHANGEL
PRAYER

SIGN OF
THE CROSS

DAY 16

Jesus said to him, "I am the way, and the truth, and the life; no one comes to the Father, but by me."

– John 14:6

The Daily Structure can be found on Pg. 22

THANKSGIVING

What three things are you thankful for today?

_____

_____

_____

_____

_____

_____

INTERCESSIONS

What three things do you want to ask for God's help?

_____

_____

_____

_____

_____

_____

JESUS CHRIST
DAY 16

JESUS CHRIST

SIGN OF
THE CROSS

INVITING THE
HOLY SPIRIT

DAILY
OFFERING
PRAYER

OUR FATHER

HAIL MARY

DOXOLOGY

ACT OF
CONTRITION

DAILY
SCRIPTURE
REFLECTION

JOURNALING

THANKSGIVING

INTERCESSIONS

FREEDOM
PRAYER

GUARDIAN
ANGEL

ST. MICHAEL
THE
ARCHANGEL
PRAYER

SIGN OF
THE CROSS

DAY 17

*For God so loved the world
that he gave his only Son, that
whoever believes in him should
not perish but have eternal life.*

– John 3:16

The Daily Structure can be found on Pg. 22

THANKSGIVING

What three things are you thankful for today?

_____

_____

_____

_____

_____

INTERCESSIONS

What three things do you want to ask for God's help?

_____

_____

_____

_____

_____

JESUS CHRIST

DAY 17

JESUS CHRIST
(DAYS 16-20)

SIGN OF
THE CROSS

INVITING THE
HOLY SPIRIT

DAILY
OFFERING
PRAYER

OUR FATHER

HAIL MARY

DOXOLOGY

ACT OF
CONTRITION

DAILY
SCRIPTURE
REFLECTION

JOURNALING

THANKSGIVING

INTERCESSIONS

FREEDOM
PRAYER

GUARDIAN
ANGEL

ST. MICHAEL
THE
ARCHANGEL
PRAYER

SIGN OF
THE CROSS

DAY 18

Jesus said to them, "I am the bread of life; he who comes to me shall not hunger, and he who believes in me shall never thirst."

– John 6:35

The Daily Structure can be found on Pg. 22

THANKSGIVING

What three things are you thankful for today?

INTERCESSIONS

What three things do you want to ask for God's help?

JESUS CHRIST

DAY 18

JESUS CHRIST
(DAYS 16-20)

SIGN OF
THE CROSS

INVITING THE
HOLY SPIRIT

DAILY
OFFERING
PRAYER

OUR FATHER

HAIL MARY

DOXOLOGY

ACT OF
CONTRITION

DAILY
SCRIPTURE
REFLECTION

JOURNALING

THANKSGIVING

INTERCESSIONS

FREEDOM
PRAYER

GUARDIAN
ANGEL

ST. MICHAEL
THE
ARCHANGEL
PRAYER

SIGN OF
THE CROSS

DAY 19

Jesus spoke to them, saying, "I am the light of the world; he who follows me will not walk in darkness, but will have the light of life."

– John 8:12

The Daily Structure can be found on Pg. 22

THANKSGIVING

What three things are you thankful for today?

_____

_____

_____

_____

_____

INTERCESSIONS

What three things do you want to ask for God's help?

_____

_____

_____

_____

_____

JESUS CHRIST

DAY 19

JESUS CHRIST
(DAYS 16-20)

**SIGN OF
THE CROSS**

**INVITING THE
HOLY SPIRIT**

**DAILY
OFFERING
PRAYER**

OUR FATHER

HAIL MARY

DOXOLOGY

**ACT OF
CONTRITION**

**DAILY
SCRIPTURE
REFLECTION**

JOURNALING

THANKSGIVING

INTERCESSIONS

**FREEDOM
PRAYER**

**GUARDIAN
ANGEL**

**ST. MICHAEL
THE
ARCHANGEL
PRAYER**

**SIGN OF
THE CROSS**

DAY 20

*Whoever confesses that Jesus
is the Son of God, God abides
in him, and he in God.*

– 1 John 4:15

The Daily Structure can be found on Pg. 22

THANKSGIVING

What three things are you thankful for today?

_____

_____

_____

_____

_____

INTERCESSIONS

What three things do you want to ask for God's help?

_____

_____

_____

_____

_____

_____

JESUS CHRIST

DAY 20

ETERNAL LIFE
(DAYS 21-25)

SIGN OF
THE CROSS

INVITING THE
HOLY SPIRIT

DAILY
OFFERING
PRAYER

OUR FATHER

HAIL MARY

DOXOLOGY

ACT OF
CONTRITION

DAILY
SCRIPTURE
REFLECTION

JOURNALING

THANKSGIVING

INTERCESSIONS

FREEDOM
PRAYER

GUARDIAN
ANGEL

ST. MICHAEL
THE
ARCHANGEL
PRAYER

SIGN OF
THE CROSS

DAY 21

For what does it profit a man, to gain the whole world and forfeit his life?

– Mark 8:36

The Daily Structure can be found on Pg. 22

THANKSGIVING

What three things are you thankful for today?

_____

_____

_____

_____

_____

_____

INTERCESSIONS

What three things do you want to ask for God's help?

_____

_____

_____

_____

_____

_____

_____

ETERNAL LIFE

DAY 21

ETERNAL LIFE
(DAYS 21-25)

DAY 22

Enter by the narrow gate; for the gate is wide and the way is easy, that leads to destruction, and those who enter by it are many. For the gate is narrow and the way is hard, that leads to life, and those who find it are few.

– Matthew 7:13-14

The Daily Structure can be found on Pg. 22

THANKSGIVING

What three things are you thankful for today?

_____

_____

_____

_____

_____

_____

INTERCESSIONS

What three things do you want to ask for God's help?

_____

_____

_____

_____

_____

_____

ETERNAL LIFE
DAY 22

ETERNAL LIFE

SIGN OF
THE CROSS

INVITING THE
HOLY SPIRIT

DAILY
OFFERING
PRAYER

OUR FATHER

HAIL MARY

DOXOLOGY

ACT OF
CONTRITION

DAILY
SCRIPTURE
REFLECTION

JOURNALING

THANKSGIVING

INTERCESSIONS

FREEDOM
PRAYER

GUARDIAN
ANGEL

ST. MICHAEL
THE
ARCHANGEL
PRAYER

SIGN OF
THE CROSS

DAY 23

Let not your hearts be troubled; believe in God, believe also in me. In my Father's house are many rooms; if it were not so, would I have told you that I go to prepare a place for you? And when I go and prepare a place for you, I will come again and will take you to myself, that where I am you may be also.

– John 14:1-3

THANKSGIVING

What three things are you thankful for today?

_____

_____

_____

_____

_____

_____

INTERCESSIONS

What three things do you want to ask for God's help?

_____

_____

_____

_____

_____

_____

_____

ETERNAL LIFE

DAY 23

ETERNAL LIFE

SIGN OF
THE CROSS

INVITING THE
HOLY SPIRIT

DAILY
OFFERING
PRAYER

OUR FATHER

HAIL MARY

DOXOLOGY

ACT OF
CONTRITION

DAILY
SCRIPTURE
REFLECTION

JOURNALING

THANKSGIVING

INTERCESSIONS

FREEDOM
PRAYER

GUARDIAN
ANGEL

ST. MICHAEL
THE
ARCHANGEL
PRAYER

SIGN OF
THE CROSS

DAY 24

*Rejoice that your names
are written in heaven.*

– Luke 10:20

The Daily Structure can be found on Pg. 22

THANKSGIVING

What three things are you thankful for today?

_____

_____

_____

_____

_____

_____

INTERCESSIONS

What three things do you want to ask for God's help?

_____

_____

_____

_____

_____

_____

_____

ETERNAL LIFE

ETERNAL
LIFE
(DAYS 21-25)

**SIGN OF
THE CROSS**

**INVITING THE
HOLY SPIRIT**

**DAILY
OFFERING
PRAYER**

OUR FATHER

HAIL MARY

DOXOLOGY

**ACT OF
CONTRITION**

**DAILY
SCRIPTURE
REFLECTION**

JOURNALING

THANKSGIVING

INTERCESSIONS

**FREEDOM
PRAYER**

**GUARDIAN
ANGEL**

**ST. MICHAEL
THE
ARCHANGEL
PRAYER**

**SIGN OF
THE CROSS**

DAY 25

*Do not lay up for yourselves
treasures on earth, where moth
and rust consume and where
thieves break in and steal, but
lay up for yourselves treasures
in heaven, where neither moth
nor rust consumes and where
thieves do not break in and
steal. For where your treasure is,
there will your heart be also.*

– Matthew 6:19-21

The Daily Structure can be found on Pg. 22

Thanksgiving

What three things are you thankful for today?

_____

_____

_____

_____

_____

_____

Intercessions

What three things do you want to ask for God's help?

_____

_____

_____

_____

_____

_____

ETERNAL LIFE

DAY 25

HOLY SPIRIT
(DAYS 26-30)

Sign of
the Cross

Inviting the
Holy Spirit

Daily
Offering
Prayer

Our Father

Hail Mary

Doxology

Act of
Contrition

Daily
Scripture
Reflection

Journaling

Thanksgiving

Intercessions

Freedom
Prayer

Guardian
Angel

St. Michael
the
Archangel
Prayer

Sign of
the Cross

Day 26

But the Counselor, the Holy Spirit, whom the Father will send in my name, he will teach you all things, and bring to your remembrance all that I have said to you.

– John 14:26

The Daily Structure can be found on Pg. 22

THANKSGIVING

What three things are you thankful for today?

_____

_____

_____

_____

_____

_____

INTERCESSIONS

What three things do you want to ask for God's help?

_____

_____

_____

_____

_____

_____

_____

HOLY SPIRIT

DAY 26

HOLY SPIRIT
(DAYS 26-30)

SIGN OF
THE CROSS

INVITING THE
HOLY SPIRIT

DAILY
OFFERING
PRAYER

OUR FATHER

HAIL MARY

DOXOLOGY

ACT OF
CONTRITION

DAILY
SCRIPTURE
REFLECTION

JOURNALING

THANKSGIVING

INTERCESSIONS

FREEDOM
PRAYER

GUARDIAN
ANGEL

ST. MICHAEL
THE
ARCHANGEL
PRAYER

SIGN OF
THE CROSS

DAY 27

But you shall receive power when the Holy Spirit has come upon you; and you shall be my witnesses in Jerusalem and in all Judea and Samaria and to the end of the earth.

– Acts 1:8

The Daily Structure can be found on Pg. 22

THANKSGIVING

What three things are you thankful for today?

_____

_____

_____

_____

_____

_____

INTERCESSIONS

What three things do you want to ask for God's help?

_____

_____

_____

_____

_____

_____

HOLY SPIRIT

DAY 27

HOLY SPIRIT
(DAYS 26-30)

DAY 28

I came to cast fire upon the earth; and would that it were already kindled!

– Luke 12:49

The Daily Structure can be found on Pg. 22

THANKSGIVING

What three things are you thankful for today?

_____

_____

_____

_____

_____

_____

INTERCESSIONS

What three things do you want to ask for God's help?

_____

_____

_____

_____

_____

_____

HOLY SPIRIT

DAY 28

HOLY SPIRIT
(DAYS 26-30)

DAY 29

John answered them all, "I baptize you with water; but he who is mightier than I is coming; he will baptize you with the Holy Spirit and with fire."

– Luke 3:16a,c

THANKSGIVING

What three things are you thankful for today?

_____

_____

_____

_____

_____

_____

INTERCESSIONS

What three things do you want to ask for God's help?

_____

_____

_____

_____

_____

_____

_____

HOLY SPIRIT

DAY 29

HOLY SPIRIT
(DAYS 26-30)

SIGN OF
THE CROSS

INVITING THE
HOLY SPIRIT

DAILY
OFFERING
PRAYER

OUR FATHER

HAIL MARY

DOXOLOGY

ACT OF
CONTRITION

DAILY
SCRIPTURE
REFLECTION

JOURNALING

THANKSGIVING

INTERCESSIONS

FREEDOM
PRAYER

GUARDIAN
ANGEL

ST. MICHAEL
THE
ARCHANGEL
PRAYER

SIGN OF
THE CROSS

DAY 30

But whoever drinks of the water that I shall give him will never thirst; the water that I shall give him will become in him a spring of water welling up to eternal life.

– John 4:14

The Daily Structure can be found on Pg. 22

THANKSGIVING

What three things are you thankful for today?

_____

_____

_____

_____

_____

INTERCESSIONS

What three things do you want to ask for God's help?

_____

_____

_____

_____

_____

_____

HOLY SPIRIT

DAY 30

DISCIPLESHIP
(DAYS 31-35)

SIGN OF
THE CROSS

INVITING THE
HOLY SPIRIT

DAILY
OFFERING
PRAYER

OUR FATHER

HAIL MARY

DOXOLOGY

ACT OF
CONTRITION

DAILY
SCRIPTURE
REFLECTION

JOURNALING

THANKSGIVING

INTERCESSIONS

FREEDOM
PRAYER

GUARDIAN
ANGEL

ST. MICHAEL
THE
ARCHANGEL
PRAYER

SIGN OF
THE CROSS

DAY 31

Every one then who hears these words of mine and does them will be like a wise man who built his house upon the rock; and the rain fell, and the floods came, and the winds blew and beat upon that house, but it did not fall, because it had been founded on the rock.

– Matthew 7:24-25

The Daily Structure can be found on Pg. 22

THANKSGIVING

What three things are you thankful for today?

_____

_____

_____

_____

_____

_____

INTERCESSIONS

What three things do you want to ask for God's help?

_____

_____

_____

_____

_____

_____

_____

DISCIPLESHIP

DAY 31

SIGN OF
THE CROSS

INVITING THE
HOLY SPIRIT

DAILY
OFFERING
PRAYER

OUR FATHER

HAIL MARY

DOXOLOGY

ACT OF
CONTRITION

DAILY
SCRIPTURE
REFLECTION

JOURNALING

THANKSGIVING

INTERCESSIONS

FREEDOM
PRAYER

GUARDIAN
ANGEL

ST. MICHAEL
THE
ARCHANGEL
PRAYER

SIGN OF
THE CROSS

DAY 32

For I was hungry and you gave me food, I was thirsty and you gave me drink, I was a stranger and you welcomed me, I was naked and you clothed me, I was sick and you visited me, I was in prison and you came to me. Then the righteous will answer him, 'Lord, when did we see thee hungry and feed thee, or thirsty and give thee drink? And when did we see thee a stranger and welcome thee, or naked and clothe thee? And when did we see thee sick or in prison and visit thee?' And the King will answer them, 'Truly, I say to you, as you did it to one of the least of these my brethren, you did it to me.'

– Matthew 25: 35-40

The Daily Structure can be found on Pg. 22

THANKSGIVING

What three things are you thankful for today?

_____

_____

_____

_____

_____

INTERCESSIONS

What three things do you want to ask for God's help?

_____

_____

_____

_____

_____

DISCIPLESHIP

DAY 32

SIGN OF
THE CROSS

INVITING THE
HOLY SPIRIT

DAILY
OFFERING
PRAYER

OUR FATHER

HAIL MARY

DOXOLOGY

ACT OF
CONTRITION

DAILY
SCRIPTURE
REFLECTION

JOURNALING

THANKSGIVING

INTERCESSIONS

FREEDOM
PRAYER

GUARDIAN
ANGEL

ST. MICHAEL
THE
ARCHANGEL
PRAYER

SIGN OF
THE CROSS

DAY 33

*You shall love the Lord your
God with all your heart, and with
all your soul, and with all your
strength, and with all your mind;
and your neighbour as yourself.*

– Luke 10:27

The Daily Structure can be found on Pg. 22

THANKSGIVING

What three things are you thankful for today?

_____

_____

_____

_____

_____

_____

INTERCESSIONS

What three things do you want to ask for God's help?

_____

_____

_____

_____

_____

_____

DISCIPLESHIP

DAY 33

SIGN OF
THE CROSS

INVITING THE
HOLY SPIRIT

DAILY
OFFERING
PRAYER

OUR FATHER

HAIL MARY

DOXOLOGY

ACT OF
CONTRITION

DAILY
SCRIPTURE
REFLECTION

JOURNALING

THANKSGIVING

INTERCESSIONS

FREEDOM
PRAYER

GUARDIAN
ANGEL

ST. MICHAEL
THE
ARCHANGEL
PRAYER

SIGN OF
THE CROSS

DAY 34

*A new commandment I give to
you, that you love one another;
even as I have loved you, that
you also love one another.*

– John 13:34

The Daily Structure can be found on Pg. 22

THANKSGIVING

What three things are you thankful for today?

_____

_____

_____

_____

_____

INTERCESSIONS

What three things do you want to ask for God's help?

_____

_____

_____

_____

_____

_____

DISCIPLESHIP

DAY 34

SIGN OF
THE CROSS

INVITING THE
HOLY SPIRIT

DAILY
OFFERING
PRAYER

OUR FATHER

HAIL MARY

DOXOLOGY

ACT OF
CONTRITION

DAILY
SCRIPTURE
REFLECTION

JOURNALING

THANKSGIVING

INTERCESSIONS

FREEDOM
PRAYER

GUARDIAN
ANGEL

ST. MICHAEL
THE
ARCHANGEL
PRAYER

SIGN OF
THE CROSS

DAY 35

Jesus said to him, "If you would be perfect, go, sell what you possess and give to the poor, and you will have treasure in heaven; and come, follow me."

– Matthew 19:21

The Daily Structure can be found on Pg. 22

167

THANKSGIVING

What three things are you thankful for today?

_____

_____

_____

_____

_____

_____

INTERCESSIONS

What three things do you want to ask for God's help?

_____

_____

_____

_____

_____

_____

_____

DISCIPLESHIP

DAY 35

OUR LADY
(DAYS 36-40)

SIGN OF
THE CROSS

INVITING THE
HOLY SPIRIT

DAILY
OFFERING
PRAYER

OUR FATHER

HAIL MARY

DOXOLOGY

ACT OF
CONTRITION

DAILY
SCRIPTURE
REFLECTION

JOURNALING

THANKSGIVING

INTERCESSIONS

FREEDOM
PRAYER

GUARDIAN
ANGEL

ST. MICHAEL
THE
ARCHANGEL
PRAYER

SIGN OF
THE CROSS

DAY 36

And Mary said, "Behold, I am the handmaid of the Lord; let it be to me according to your word."

– Luke 1:38

The Daily Structure can be found on Pg. 22

THANKSGIVING

What three things are you thankful for today?

_____

_____

_____

_____

_____

_____

INTERCESSIONS

What three things do you want to ask for God's help?

_____

_____

_____

_____

_____

_____

OUR LADY

DAY 36

OUR LADY

SIGN OF
THE CROSS

INVITING THE
HOLY SPIRIT

DAILY
OFFERING
PRAYER

OUR FATHER

HAIL MARY

DOXOLOGY

ACT OF
CONTRITION

DAILY
SCRIPTURE
REFLECTION

JOURNALING

THANKSGIVING

INTERCESSIONS

FREEDOM
PRAYER

GUARDIAN
ANGEL

ST. MICHAEL
THE
ARCHANGEL
PRAYER

SIGN OF
THE CROSS

DAY 37

And Mary said, "My soul magnifies the Lord, and my spirit rejoices in God my Saviour."

– Luke 1:46-47

The Daily Structure can be found on Pg. 22

THANKSGIVING
What three things are you thankful for today?

_____

_____

_____

_____

_____

INTERCESSIONS
What three things do you want to ask for God's help?

_____

_____

_____

_____

_____

_____

OUR LADY
Day 37

OUR LADY

SIGN OF
THE CROSS

INVITING THE
HOLY SPIRIT

DAILY
OFFERING
PRAYER

OUR FATHER

HAIL MARY

DOXOLOGY

ACT OF
CONTRITION

DAILY
SCRIPTURE
REFLECTION

JOURNALING

THANKSGIVING

INTERCESSIONS

FREEDOM
PRAYER

GUARDIAN
ANGEL

ST. MICHAEL
THE
ARCHANGEL
PRAYER

SIGN OF
THE CROSS

DAY 38

*But Mary kept all these things,
pondering them in her heart.*

– Luke 2:19

The Daily Structure can be found on Pg. 22

THANKSGIVING

What three things are you thankful for today?

_____

_____

_____

_____

_____

_____

INTERCESSIONS

What three things do you want to ask for God's help?

_____

_____

_____

_____

_____

_____

_____

OUR LADY

Day 38

OUR LADY

SIGN OF
THE CROSS

INVITING THE
HOLY SPIRIT

DAILY
OFFERING
PRAYER

OUR FATHER

HAIL MARY

DOXOLOGY

ACT OF
CONTRITION

DAILY
SCRIPTURE
REFLECTION

JOURNALING

THANKSGIVING

INTERCESSIONS

FREEDOM
PRAYER

GUARDIAN
ANGEL

ST. MICHAEL
THE
ARCHANGEL
PRAYER

SIGN OF
THE CROSS

DAY 39

*His mother said to the servants,
"Do whatever he tells you."*

– John 2:5

The Daily Structure can be found on Pg. 22

THANKSGIVING

What three things are you thankful for today?

_____

_____

_____

_____

_____

_____

INTERCESSIONS

What three things do you want to ask for God's help?

_____

_____

_____

_____

_____

_____

OUR LADY

DAY 39

OUR LADY
(DAYS 36-40)

SIGN OF
THE CROSS

INVITING THE
HOLY SPIRIT

DAILY
OFFERING
PRAYER

OUR FATHER

HAIL MARY

DOXOLOGY

ACT OF
CONTRITION

DAILY
SCRIPTURE
REFLECTION

JOURNALING

THANKSGIVING

INTERCESSIONS

FREEDOM
PRAYER

GUARDIAN
ANGEL

ST. MICHAEL
THE
ARCHANGEL
PRAYER

SIGN OF
THE CROSS

DAY 40

When Jesus saw his mother, and the disciple whom he loved standing near, he said to his mother, "Woman, behold, your son!" Then he said to the disciple, "Behold, your mother!" And from that hour the disciple took her to his own home.

– John 19:26-27

The Daily Structure can be found on Pg. 22

THANKSGIVING

What three things are you thankful for today?

_____

_____

_____

_____

_____

_____

INTERCESSIONS

What three things do you want to ask for God's help?

_____

_____

_____

_____

_____

_____

_____

OUR LADY

DAY 40

TREASURE IN HEAVEN BOOKLET

The *Treasure in Heaven* booklet is a simple and powerful prayer guide in a convenient pocket-sized package. It contains the same 40-day, 10 minutes a day prayer challenge without the journaling portion. Perfect for when you are on the go, and for distributing at events.

Orders within Canada, requiring shipping, must be ordered in increments of 25 *(+ shipping & handling)*.

International orders, including the U.S.A., requiring shipping, must be ordered in increments of 100 *(+ shipping and handling)*.

To order additional copies, call our office:
1-866-885-8824 (Toll free)

Or send your address and requests by mail to:
Companions of the Cross
199 Bayswater Avenue
Ottawa, Ontario, Canada K1Y 2G5

We would love to hear stories of how Treasure in Heaven has affected your life, or the life of someone you know. Send your stories and feedback to:
tih@companionscross.org

Front Cover Image: Bryan Minear (unsplash.com/@bryanminear)

 # COMPANIONS OF THE CROSS

We are a community of Catholic priests inviting people to know Jesus and empowering them to share Jesus.

> *"I see the Church waking up and coming explosively alive to the point where it, with the power of the Holy Spirit, will shake the earth and the nations with its dynamic presence."* – Fr. Bob Bedard, CC

Our priests preach the Word of God with passion, celebrate the sacraments with devotion, and lead with confidence.

As Companions of the Cross we root ourselves in:

Brotherhood
A LIFE OF TRUE BROTHERHOOD
We base ourselves on the model of Jesus and his disciples, who lived together, ministered together, and supported one another.

Spirituality
A SPIRITUALITY OF GOD'S POWER AND WISDOM
Jesus's death on the cross and resurrection saved the world. Therefore, we fully commit ourselves to him; seek his will in all we do; and trust in his power to carry it out.

Mission
A MISSION OF EVANGELIZATION AND RENEWAL
We invite all people into an initial and ongoing encounter with Jesus. As we are transformed by his love, we bring about authentic renewal in the Church and the world.

Follow Us:

199 Bayswater Avenue, Ottawa, ON Canada K1Y 2G5 | **1.866.885.8824**
info@companionscross.org | **WWW.COMPANIONSCROSS.ORG**

Do Whatever
He tells you

-JOHN 2:5